CIMME.....

OR
Eurasians and Their Future

BY CEDRIC DOVER

An Anglo Indian Heritage Book

Warning

CIMMERII?

OR
Eurasians and Their Future

BY

CEDRIC DOVER

Sometime: Assistant temporarily In charge of Etymology,
Zoological Survey of India;
Assistant Secretary, Asiatic Society of Bengal;
Assistant, Raffles and Federated Malaya State Museums;
Assistant Entomologist, Department of Agriculture.
SS And F.M.S; Ostreoculturist. Federated Malaya
State (Fisheries Department);
Editor, 'The New Outlook",
" Huxley's 'Palmer's Annual", and " The Klymcan ";
Author of The Kingdom of Earth", and
Of numerous scientific and popular
Papers and memoirs.

Simon Wallenberg Press

The Anglo Indian Heritage

Cimmerii? Or Eurasians and Their Future by Cedric Dover is the fourth book in the Anglo Indian Heritage series.

The Others are:

Herbert Alick Stark 'Hostages To India

Britain's Betrayal in India: The Story of the Anglo Indian Community

These are the Anglo Indians by Reginald Maher

The books are called the Anglo Indian Heritage books as they chronicle the rich and colourful history of the Anglo Indian Community.

This small community has had outstanding achievements at every level of society for hundreds of years but that record of achievement has been hidden, passed over or co-opted as British and Indian History.

These Books are an attempt to fairly represent the history of the community by works by Anglo Indians themselves.

Cedric Dover (1904-1961)

Born in Calcutta, India, Cedric Dover an Anglo Indian studied intergroup relations (a type of sociology), later researching and teaching in the field as a Professor of Zoology in India and Malaysia and then as visiting professor of anthropology at Fisk University in the United States.

He continued his academic work in America as professor of intergroup relations at the New School in New York City. The problems of people of color and the cultural achievements of oppressed peoples were his lifelong concern.

He wrote many books in social and ethnic studies, including Half-Caste, Know this of Race, Hell in the Sunshine, Features in the Arrow and Brown Phoenix.

Later in life Dover edited an anthology of black art in the United States, American Negro Art (1960). Art historians suggest that the pioneering work of Dover and contemporaries contributed to an understanding of a "black aesthetic" in cultural production

And wilt thou tremble so, my heart, When the mighty breathe on thee? And shall thy light like this depart; Away ! It cannot be.

H. L. V. Derozio (Eurasian poet)

Let us, the Children of the Night, Put off the cloak that hides the scar! Let us be Children of the Light, And tell the ages what we are!

Edwin A. Robinson (Negro poet)

(The difference between Eurasian and Negro Independence is shown in these verses. The Eurasians need more of the aggressive Negro spirit.)

FOREWORD

A well-known writer once told me it was wise to start an essay with a text. I may be wrong, but I believe him right. And for my text I would choose an Anglo-Saxon definition of the Eurasian.

There are many. But the definition (pronounced by Corporal Dekker in Bruce's novel "The Eurasian "[1]) which follows is so concise, pungent and unique that it demands consideration. It goes like this - "Do you know what an Yewraysian is. Cherry? He'm the half part of a nigger; but not the twentieth part of a man. Never you trust an Yewraysian, Cherry, if you meet one. He'll twist in your fingers like a false tool; and lucky you, if you'm not wounded. A nigger is a devil, most times. But an Yewraysian is not a proper human being."

I believe these words express the general attitude of the white races towards the results of

---

1 BRUCE, Henry, Novelist. The Eurasian.
Publisher/year John Long: London, 1913.

their own amativeness. Is it fair? Is it right?
Three hundred thousand Eurasians in the British Empire are constantly asking themselves
these questions. And those who know the an-
swers are frankly resentful; those who do not are
compelled to accept the circumstances as they
are, but not without a secret or subconscious
resentment.

It is a resentment which is gradually being
forced on the White World; and its visionaries
recognise in the Eurasians a serious problem
of administration in the East. It is, therefore,
as an attempt to foster a proper appreciation of
the Eurasian community and its problems, both
in the Eurasians themselves and in the people
of other communities and nationalities, and to
quicken a mutual understanding, that I offer
this essay—penned under the searching scrutiny
of biological and historical facts. It is in consequence freer from those extravagances which
characterize the writings of the critics and supporters of these unhappy people.

Perhaps I am unduly ambitious. But if these
pages do no more they will at least support Lord
Oliver's opinion—an opinion of very wide signifi-
cance—that " so far as there survives in a mixed

race the racial body of each of its parents, so far it is a superior human being, or rather, I would say, potentially a more competent vehicle of humanity."

C. D.

Calcutta: March, 1929.

Chapter I

CIMMERII ?

OR EURASIANS AND THEIR FUTURE

The novelists—not even our moderns, like John Paris or Somerset Maugham—have never been kind to the Eurasian. Bruce, for instance, makes his principal character a weak, drug-addicted, illegitimate son of a prostitute by a British officer of the Indian Civil Service. But novelists reflect the opinions of their age and in particular their own race. And the ordinary European generally believes that Eurasians are the result of temporary weaknesses in an unaccustomed climate. While he is not entirely wrong, he is certainly not right.

The origin of mixed communities in the East will prove this. We could go back more than two thousand years to the time when Alexander, thirsting for knowledge and power, set out to conquer the world. We could recount his travels and conquests; his determination to fuse the nations of Asia and Greece into one harmonious whole. We could tell of the rewards, with the women of the country; of Alexander's own Asiatic wives and (who can say how many?) mistresses.

We could go further and discuss the relationship between the Greeks and the great Empire of Chandragupta Maury a, a relationship cemented by the marriage of the Indian King with the daughter of Seleukos Nikator. We could legitimately advance the supposition that the great Asoka, grandson of Chandragupta, was an Eurasian. We could also reasonably suppose that the influence of India on Greek culture, and the Grecian influence on ancient Indian art, was due mainly to the presence of a mixed community, which broke down the barriers of language and prejudice.

But these are subjects which form a research in themselves. They have an academic, rather than a practical, interest for the Eurasians of to-day. Let us turn, therefore, as a more concrete example, to the origin of the present Eurasian or Anglo-Indian community in India. It dates back to the early sixteenth century, the era of Portuguese power in India.

EURASIANS AND THEIR FUTURE

Sagacious and religious rulers as they were, the Portuguese sought to produce a permanent Portuguese (and Catholic) community in India by encouraging the marriage of pure Lusitanians with Indians.

While the Portuguese remained in power the large mixed population which grew up justified the expectations of its sponsors, but when the rulers were, forced to cede their interests to the Dutch and English their hybrid children rapidly lost their Portuguese distinctiveness. Deprived of the patronage of their fathers, the Luso-Indians soon became absorbed in the maternal stock, or by marriage with English soldiers partly lost themselves in the British-Indian community.

To-day, very few Luso-Indians can be found who can trace their ancestry to an European Portuguese, and all that remains of their European origin is their staunch Catholicism and their lofty names, including that of the great Albuquerque himself. The mixed Lusitanian community of Malacca in the Straits Settlements, sponsored by St. Francis Xavier, has shared a similar fate.

When the English insinuated themselves into India, the factories of the East India Company sprang up with such rapidity that the assistance of the Luso-Indians was enlisted. Continued communal intercourse led inevitably to marriage, especially as the social customs and religion of the hybrid community closely approached that of the servants of the Company.

It is unfortunate that the Luso-Indians were confirmed Catholics, relentless in their attitude towards other faiths, while the Britishers were Protestants. Unfortunate, because marital harmony involved the conversion of the Protestants, a process viewed with great disfavor in Puritan England. Thus were the germs of prejudice against intermarriage sewn.

The problem partly solved itself. The demand for Luso-Indian womanhood exceeded the supply. Polyandry, Concubinage, or marriage with pure Indian women was the only remedies —and Christianity only permitted the last. The Court of Directors of the Company, realizing that the sexual urge was more powerful than legislation, thus addressed the President of Madras in 1678: . "The marriage of our soldiers to the native women of Fort St. George is a matter of such consequence to posterity that we shall be content to encourage it with some expense, and have been thinking for the future to appoint a pagoda to be paid to the mother of any child, that shall hereafter be born of any such future marriage, upon the day the child is christened, if you think this small encouragement will increase the number of such marriages."

So, first by Christian zeal and then by a deliberate diplomatic policy, the Eurasians of India came into being. And it should be obvious that where permanent relationships are contracted the same cultural level is sought. In Bengal, Prof. P. C. Mahalanobis - *[2] has recently provided very striking proof in support of this argument.

He analyzed statistically the anthropometrical results obtained from investigations on thirty Bengal castes and compared them with the results obtained from a study of two hundred Eurasians in Bengal. He found that on the Indian side the Eurasians most closely resembled the Bengal Brahmans, socially the highest class. He writes: "So far as the present analysis goes we see that intermixture between Europeans and Indians occurred more frequently among the

2 *Analysis of Race Mixture in Bengal." Journal of the Asiatic Society of Bengal, new series, xxiii, No. 3, 1928.
-

higher castes than the lower. Evidently cultural status played a considerable part in determining Indo-European unions."

The facts of history are here supported by the considered opinion of a trained biometrician. Are we right then in asserting that the mothers of all half castes are of the culturally inferior race? Are we right in stigmatizing the Eurasians as bastards?

Chapter II

While every intelligent person must relinquish the theory that the Eurasians of India are of lowly, lustful origin, it must also be admitted that Concubinage did exist, though this does not prove " that in every case the half-caste races have arisen as the result of illicit relations between the men of the superior and the women of the inferior race."[3] - How could it be otherwise when the British were the rulers of the land and women were to be had as easily as cattle?

But religious and social prejudice soon caused the disappearance of the results of these unions. The children of the lower class Englishmen and native mistresses, deprived of the benefits of pecuniary stability and social sanction, soon lost themselves in the Indian population, while the offspring of more fortunately situated fathers were sent to England seldom to return.

---

3 *See Reuter, The Mulatto in the United States (Boston, 1918).*
It may be noted in passing that the children of the legitimate unions of officials were also sent to England, thus depriving the Eurasian community of those who would have added to their elite.

To-day, therefore, the bastard only exists here and there, Just as the bastard exists in all countries, and, in any case, the religious fanaticism which created the bastard (an innocent biological expression made cruel by Christian society) an outcast, no longer exists among the true intelligentsia of our age.

Let us continue to trace the beginnings of anti-Eurasian prejudice in India. Almost till the beginning of the nineteenth century, the Eurasian community had enjoyed complete social and political freedom. Its members filled posts of important in every branch of the Company's services, particularly in the Army. Indeed, it may well be questioned whether England would ever have gained her present dominance over India without the aid of the community she affects to despise.

As an Eurasian historian[4]* writes, these were the years of their prosperity; the days of adversity were at hand. The first signs of repression

---

4 *Mr. H. A. Stark, late of the Indian Educational Service, to whose splendid Hostages to India {Calcutta, 1926) 1 am indebted for much of my historical information. In this work the story of the Eurasians in India is told at greater length, and with more pathos, than is possible here.

came in 1786, when Eurasian orphans were prohibited from proceeding to England to complete their education; it reached a climax in 1791 when, by a standing order of the Court of Directors of the East India Company, persons with Indian blood in their veins were debarred from the Civil, Military and Marine Services of the Company.

The reason for this change of front of the very Company which had deliberately fostered the growth of the Eurasian community is not far to seek. India was better known; the pioneering days were practically over; and financial security was more easily obtainable there than at Home. Small wonder that the shareholders of the Company sought to take a more intimate part in the exploitation of India by reserving the vacancies in the Company's services for their own relations!

Fortunately for their greed, the years of Eurasian repression coincided with the establishment of the Black Republic at Hayti, where the tyranny of the Spaniards against the mulattoes had rightly resulted in a victory for the oppressed. Would the tragedy of Hayti be reenacted in India? Would the Eurasians rise up and, at the head of their Indian relations, crush the foothold the British were gaining? Fear of an Eurasian revolt and the analogy of mulatto victories provided a wonderful basis for anti-Eurasian propaganda— and it was worked for all it was worth.

What Justice, what sense of parental and moral obligations could be expected from the England of that era? An England in which semi-nude women worked, literally as beasts of burden, in the mines; an England in which thousands of half-starved children died every year through the most cruel forms of menial labour and the indifference of both parents and the State.

Chapter III

We have seen that as the Christian religion and the desire for national aggrandizement were instrumental in bringing a mixed community into being in India, so these same factors contributed to its social and economic repression.

With the renewal of the Company's Charter in 1833, whereby the order prohibiting English women from proceeding to India was rescinded, another factor, more subtle but equally powerful, made itself felt in the war against the Eurasian. It was a biological factor this time—the instinct of self and race preservation, an instinct of which the mothers of the race are naturally more conscious than the fortuitous males.

Two years after the renewal of the Charter the overland route to India was opened; the voyage became cheaper, quicker and more comfortable; and large numbers of ambitious Englishmen poured into the country, bringing with them their wives, or sending for them at the earliest opportunity. These women instinctively saw the danger to themselves and their female relations and friends of intermarriages. The surest way to discourage this was to taboo the Eurasian—and it does not take a woman long to have her way.

The far-seeing mothers of the English race also saw that the social ostracism of the Eurasian would make it easier for their own men folk to obtain preferential treatment. The plums of the Company's services were no longer entirely reserved for Englishmen, the renewed Charter having decreed that no British Subject " shall, by reason of his religion, place of birth, descent, colour or any of them be disabled from holding any place, office or employment under the said Company," though the higher posts had to be filled by recruitment in England.

The women of England, however, continued the work of destruction which legislation had inaugurated but failed to maintain. Forty years of active repression had weakened the strength of the community; social prejudice now made it impossible for them to hold out against the English in India, or to recoup themselves by frequent marriages with Englishmen of means and position.

The few fortunate Eurasians who could afford to join the higher grades pf the Public Services by enlistment in England soon found that they were

the victims of preferential treatment and social
ostracism; the majority could not afford the expense of study abroad.

So, the community which had served the Father-
land so well degenerated into a community of
clerks, railway-men and telegraphists, forced to
be content with employment in the subordinate
grades of the Company's services. Oppression
had won. But the thoughtful statesman knows
that the final victory rests always with the oppressed.

Chapter IV

Some of the main causes of the inferiority of
the Euro-Indians will now be understood.
Yet this community had its days of prosperity.
The Eurasians further east were conceived, and
brought up in adversity. Is it surprising that
they are on an even lower plane than their cous-
ins in India?

Consider their origin briefly. They come into
being much later than the East Indians, at a
time when prejudice against the half-caste was
already well-established, if it was not actually at
its zenith. Moreover, in the England of that day
women were regarded either as instruments for
the satisfaction of male passions or as beasts of
burden—or both.

The type of men attracted by the Colonies were
not the type of men who had originally exploited
India. Racial prejudice and the moral outlook of
their time, combined in causing them to treat
native women with even greater bestiality than
women were being treated at Home. Listen to

EURASIANS AND THEIR FUTURE

Justin McCarthy on this point: "Women actually with child had been scourged with as many as one hundred and seventy lashes. Women had been stripped, tied up to a post and left there naked through a whole day, writhing under a tropical sun and with a flogging inflicted at stated intervals. Half-caste women, almost as white as English women, were frequently to be identified by the brand upon their breasts."

Mercifully, the offspring of such lustful beasts have usually become absorbed in the maternal stock. The Eurasians of the Far East who still exist to-day are the children of more humane, more intelligent, fathers who, by marriage within the community, augmented occasionally by marriages with pure whites, have preserved their identity.

They have grown up in an atmosphere of the most intense prejudice, unsupported even by the small measure of protection afforded to the East Indians, but they have survived. And the novelist should remember that even in human society only the fittest survive.

How intense col our-prejudice is in the Far East
may be guessed from these remarks by Dr. H. N.
Ridley, F.R.S., *[5] (one of the few distinguished
scientists Malaya has known) in a paper on
the Eurasian problem read before the Straits
Philosophical Society in 1895 "Taking the race
as a whole they are weak in body, short-lived,
deficient in energy and feeble in morals. Even a
little admixture of native blood seems to result
in an individual who possesses the bad qualities
of both races."

In the discussion which followed, his outstanding supporter was Mr. Hugh Fort, who declared
that the Eurasian was contemptible and unable
to pit himself against a robust coolie.

As a student of biology I quote these remarks
of one of the greatest systematic botanists alive
with a certain reluctance. I shall disprove their
accuracy in later sections. At present it will suf-
fice to say that if one of the most distinguished

---

5 * Copies in the public libraries at Penang and Singapore. lady
Drummond Hay's article on the Eurasian Problem in the Sphere,
Feb. 4. 1928, (reprinted in the Anglo-Indian Citizen) gives a vivid
picture of the prejudice suffered by Eurasians, even those of high
social standing.

men in Malaya at that time could, without the deliberation which even a minor scientific problem involves, lightly dismiss the Eurasian in these words before a gathering of the intelligentsia, then the attitude of less enlightened Europeans towards the mixed blood race of that country may well be imagined, for who is really more contemptible? The inferior Eurasian or his white wards? The philosopher will know the answer.

Chapter V

We have heard the evidence of history. What has biology to say of the despised Eurasian? Does it prove him fundamentally inferior, or is his inferiority an environmental result?

It is a popular fallacy that the hybrid is intrinsically inferior to either parent. That the agriculturist, the horticulturist, the cattle-breeder and the experimental geneticist have repeatedly disproved it*[6] matters little to the critic who lives by criticising. Where humanity is concerned even distinguished biologists are supporters of this theory, the weight of their names adding credence to their opinions, and providing apparently erudite arguments for their less learned followers.

---

6 *'See, for example, such works as East and Jones' Inbreeding and Out breeding (Monographs in Experimental Biology, Philadelphia, 1919); Castle's Genetics and Eugenics Harvard University Press, 1916); Finot's Race Prejudice London, 1906); and The Mechanism of Mendelian Heredity (revised edition, New York. 1926) by Morgan and others. For a scientist's contribution to the popular theory see The Menace of Colour (London, 1925) by Prof. Gregory.

EURASIANS AND THEIR FUTURE

Still even biologists are only human. And, while it is easy to study life below the human scale in a calm, dispassionate manner, it is difficult to

-estimate our fellow-men without permitting preconceived notions, born of religious, social, or political bias, to taint our conclusions.

So we may excuse Dr. Ridley's opinions (after all he was not speaking ex cathedra) for the Eurasian of Malaya has proved them wrong; we may smile at the belief of E. D. Cope (one of America's most famous scientists) that the mulatto is inferior to the Negro, for the Negro owes his rapidly advancing position mainly to the efforts of mulattoes, among whom Booker T. Washington and E. B. du Bois are conspicuous examples ;*[7] we may dismiss as antiquated Dr. Paul Broca's work on Human Hybridity (1864) in which he states that the half-castes of Java are defective in intelligence and fecundity and are unable to breed beyond the third generation, for a flourishing Eurasian population in Java, in no wise inferior to its Dutch progenitors, gives the lie to these statements.

---

7 *In The Mulatto in the United Stales (Boston, 1918) Heater proven beyond doubt that nearly all the prominent colored men in America are mulattoes.

CIMMERII?

Let us examine some of these pseudo-biological accusations against the Eurasian. He is weak in body, says Dr. Ridley and other writers. We must admit, of course, that he is frequently less robust than the European, but this state is obviously not the result of his mixed blood; it is caused by his environment.

How can we expect the Eurasian, born and brought up in a tropical climate, his condition aggravated by economic distress, to be as stalwart as an Anglo-Saxon? That he is potentially as strong as any Westerner is proved by the physique of those Eurasian boys who have been entirely educated in the hill schools of India.

In fact, it may well be claimed that he is potentially even stronger than the European, for I know from my own experience of India and the Far East that he has excelled the European in every game in which stamina and alertness counts for more than sheer weight.

In Malaya, for example, a hockey team consisting entirely of Eurasian lads, none of whom had played hockey for more than three seasons (two of them had never played hockey before !), won thirty-eight out of forty matches against Euro-

pean and Asiatic clubs. On the two occasions
on which they were beaten they were not at full
strength, the winners, composed as they were of
public school and regimental players. University
Blues, and even ex-English internationals, being
two of the finest teams in Malaya.

In India, Eurasian hockey elevens are the leading exponents of the game. The Indian Olympic
team, which recently astonished all Europe, was
managed by Mr. A. B. Rosser, an Eurasian who
is an outstanding personality in Indian sport.
It contained nine Eurasians out of the thirteen
players who went from India, and it was even
felt that some of the Indians (great players
though they were) had been included as a con-
cession to Indian sentiment. That this feeling
was not entirely without justification is proved
by the fact that the Olympic eleven was defeated
at Bombay by a scratch team of Eurasian lads.

So much for hockey. In every other branch of
sport (except polo and hunting, which they cannot afford) Eurasians all over the East are holding their own with Europeans and Asiatics. In
boxing, which they have only taken up recently,
Eurasians have defeated some of the best men
in the British Army. These are not irresponsible

statements. Anyone who knows the East will testify to their accuracy; anyone can prove it for themselves.

Strictly scientific evidence also is not wanting to disprove this libel on Eurasian physique. Prof., P. C. Mahalanobis* has analysed statistically the male stature of two hundred Eurasians measured in Calcutta. His comparative researches indicate that the Eurasians are superior in stature to other natives of Bengal, and that there is little to choose between them and Europeans. Prof. Mahalanobis[8]* work is still in progress and, from conversations I have had with him, H am convinced it will completely support my contention that the critics of Eurasian physique are either ignorant of scientific methods, or have willfully departed from them.

After all illogical prejudices are hard to eradicate. And it pleases the European to describe Eurasians as physical weaklings.

---

8 * *Anthropological Observations on the Anglo-Indians of Calcutta. Part I. Analysis of Male Stature. Records of the Indian Museum, xxiii, April, 1922.*

Chapter VI

The only certainty about the Eurasian is his uncertainty, says Mr. Bruce; he is deficient in energy, says Dr. Ridley; he is a coward, say the novelists. But listen to this record of Eurasian services to the East India Company.

As Mr. Stark writes: " They gallantly fought under Clive at Arcot, Sriramgaon and Trichinopoly in the Second Kamatic War; and at Wandiwash under Eyre Coote. They perished in the Black Hole of Calcutta. They were in the line of battle at Plassey. They participated in the campaigns which put an end to French aspirations in India. They were massacred with their English comrades by the soldiery of Mir Kassim at Patna (1763), fought in the battle of Buxar (1764), and were present at the capture of Allahabad. They took part in the Rohilla War (1772). the First Maratha War (1775) and in the Second Mysore War (1780).**

When the Maratha Wars were resumed, Eurasians fought side by side with the very nation which had so recently cast them out of its army. Indeed, they even left the services of Indian Chiefs, with whom they had enlisted, to rejoin the British.

Vickers, Oodd and Ryan, three heroes in Holkar's army, suffered a cruel death at the Maharajah's hands because they insisted on answering the call of their British blood. Yet this gallant community was once again cast out of the British Army on the termination of the wars.

Fifty years had not elapsed since their dismissal when, in the Sepoy Mutiny, they again showed their uncertainty, their laziness, their cowardice by literally saving India. Brendish*[9] saved the Punjab, Hearsay Calcutta, Forgett Bombay. The boys of the Martiniere College defended the Lucknow Residency; on every hand the despised half-caste showed his heroism, his disregard for danger. Fifteen years ago the Eurasians once again proved their worth when, from every country in the East, they flocked in thousands to the British lines in Europe, in Asia Minor, and in Africa. The so-called Anglo-Indians alone pro-

---

9 * *It is typical of some English historians that in Fitchctt's Tale of the Indian Mutiny this gallant Eurasian is described an "English boy " some idea of the strength of the Anglo-Indian regiments are given in The Anglo-Indian Force (Allahabad, 1918).*

vided a larger percentage of men than any other Colony or Dependency in the British Empire.

But enough. We have proved that the Eurasian community is second to none in stamina, in courage, in energy, in steadfastness of purpose; that in the individuals in whom these traits do exist they are the results not of inheritance, not of the supposed conflict of mixed blood, but of environmental adversity.

Chapter VII

The intellectual and other potentialities of the Eurasian community can be measured from the galaxy of famous men which it has produced in spite of its disabilities. Would you have great soldiers? Then study the lives of Col. Jas. Skinner, C. B., Col. Henry Forster, C. B., General Jones, Major Hyder Young Hearsay, Col. Stevenson and Major Naime.

Would you have statesmen? The life of Ricketts shows that he would have shone as a parliamentarian. Would you have educationalists, scholars, writers, poets and artists ? Names are difficult to select, but one may mention Wale Byrne and Peter Carstairs as educationalists, Stark, Moreno, Madge and Upson as scholars and writers, Charles Pote as a portrait painter of reputation. Special reference must be made to Henry Louis Vivian Derozio, who in his teens was a Professor of English, who as a teacher, journalist, philosopher and poet left behind him an indelible impression on the culture of Bengal, though he died before he was twenty-three.

Would you have doctors and scientists? The Community can point with pride to Lt.-Col. H. A. J. Gidney, I.M.S. (Retd.) whose accomplishments in ophthalmic surgery have been unfortunately overshadowed by his sacrifice in relinquishing this career for the less lucrative field of Eurasian; politics.

It can also recall the reputation of Drs. Briton, Lumsden, Chambers and Wallace, and dwell with satisfaction on the work of Lt.-Col. A. E. Baptist, M.B.E., Assistant Director of the School of Tropical Medicine, and C. A. Paiva, late Entomologist in the Indian Museum.

Would you have men of business and administrative ability? They are legion, but the names of Sir George Kellner of the Military Department, Government of India, of John Palmer, who lent the Nizam of Hyderabad a fabulous sum of money, and of James Kyd, Master Ship-builder, after whom the Calcutta docks (which he built) and an important suburb of Calcutta are named, stand out prominently from the rest.

CIMMERII?

Turning to Eurasian women would you admire beauty, as well as brains? Then consider the portraits of Kitty Kirkpatrick, the original Bluminc of Carlyle's Sartor Resartus; of Madame Grand, who in her day dominated Calcutta society and later married the great Prince Talleyrand; of the masterly wife of Dupleix, a French Governor-General in India, who was the force behind her husband's administration. Of other renowned women the fame of Madame Alice Gomes, the Eurasian Patti, is most easily recalled.

I have deliberately refrained from referring to the long list of noble names which occur among Eurasians, for kinship with the decaying aristocracies of Europe is no measure of potential greatness.

Yet, for the satisfaction of those whom monarchical constitutions have rendered enamoured of the nobility, it may be mentioned that the Gardner family, the second .Earl of Liverpool, once Prime Minister of England, the half-brother of Lord Roberts, and the descendants of the reigning house of Bourbon, and of the Earl of Duffus, have to acknowledge the Indian blood which flows in their veins. Many other famous or noble names come to my mind, but their owners prefer the obscurity of retirement as English gentlemen.[10]*

I have drawn these examples from the annals of Edwardian history. But we can go still further afield to prove that the half-caste is not intellectually inferior to the pure white.

In the short century of their existence the Eurasians of the Straits Settlements have produced an imposing array of men and women of whom they may be justifiably proud ;*[11]it is truly said that Brazil never produced a statesman who was not a mulatto; it cannot be denied that the Ne-

10 * For chapter and verse the reader may refer to such works as Fraser's Military Memoirs of Lt.-Col. fast. Shin-net. C.B.. (London, 1857); Hearse's The Hearsay's, Four Generations of an Anglo-Indian Family; Compton's A Particular Account of the European Military Adventures of Hindustan from 1784 to 1803 (London, 1892); Edwards' Henry Derozio, the Eurasian Poet, Teacher and journalist (Calcutta, 1884); Bradley Bin's Poems of Henry Louis Vivian Derozio (Oxford University Press, 1923); Madge's " When Generals Married Begums" in the Statesman, Calcutta, Feb., II, 1906; Stark and Madge's East Indian Worthies (Calcutta, 1892); Moreno's The Call to Arms for Anglo-Indians (Calcutta, 1916), and "Some Anglo-Indian Terms and Origins" in The Indian Athenaeum, Calcutta, August, 1923 (also published in the Proceedings of the Indian Historical Records Commission, V, Calcutta, 1923); Dunn's " An Anglo-Indian Romance " in the Calcutta Review, Jan., 1919; and The Indo-Briton, an anonymous work published by the Missionary Society at Bombay in 1849.

11 * See Carlos, in Makepeace. Brooke and Braddell's. One Hundred Years of Singapore (London, 1921), Vol. 1, page 363. Vol. 11. page 294.

groes of America owe their wealth and their new learning to mulattoes.

But no useful purpose can be served by further enlargement. We have now to face the accusation that the greatest men among the so-called mixed races cannot compare with the great intellectuals of Europe. We must admit its truth. But can we expect from a young and proscribed people a Shakespeare, a Darwin, or a Newton? Should we ask more of them than the men they have already produced, men who in any country in the world would have earned a place among the lesser intellectuals? Where are the intellectual contributions of Britain in the first thousand years of her existence?

Two other arguments may be dismissed here: the short-life and the immorality of the Eurasians. The first cannot be disputed. The Eurasians are generally shorter-lived than Europeans living in their own countries, but here again this is not an affliction of hybridity but of environment.

Can we expect a man, toiling day after day in the cruel heat of the tropics, disillusioned by social prejudice, unable to afford a holiday, to

live as long as an European? That potentially
the Eurasian community is not inferior in this
respect is proved by the long life of those of its
members who can afford good food, intellectual
interests, and periodic holidays in Europe or the
hills.

We cannot call the second accusation wrong; we
may not call it right. We can only treat with contempt a statement which attempts to create the
impression that half-castes alone are immoral,
or at least more immoral than their white ancestors.

I maintain that in any part of the world the half-
caste is no more a blasphemer, no more a drunk-
ard, no more a pervert, no more a brothel-mon-
ger, than the pure bred white or black. Indeed, it
may be claimed that if his morals are not intrinsically superior, they are at least practically so,
in as much as morality is for him an economic
necessity.

The Eurasian, for example, marries young (
and, in spite of allegations against his fecundity,
produces more children than he ought to do)
and his whole attention is soon concentrated on
the soul-destroying process of making two ends

meet—the surest enemy of indulgence known.

Anyone who really knows both East and West
will admit me right. Let him who does not prove
me wrong.

Chapter VIII

We have dealt with pseudo-biological twaddle and the criticisms of the write-to-please-the-public authors. But serious students of -mixed races have been no less unfair to the Eurasian. Their opinions have been admirably summed up (and ignorantly perpetuated) by Reuter in his work on the mulatto in the United States and other mixed breeds. He writes:

"Physically the Eurasians are slight and weak. They are naturally indolent and will enter into no employment requiring exertion or labour. This lack of energy is correlated with an incapacity for organisation. They will not assume burdensome responsibilities, but they make passable clerks where only routine labour is required. Lacking in manhood they are wily, untrustworthy and untruthful. They are lacking in independence, and are for ever begging for special favors. They recklessly resign from any and every post when, for some reason or without reason, their feelings are hurt. The girls, in some cases at least, are sold into prostitution. They are despised by the ruling whites and hated by the natives."

CIMMERII?

We have already considered some of these criticisms, but Mr. Reuter deserves a special answer. To his first argument we reply that at least ninety per cent, of the Eurasian community is employed in departments, such as the railways, where hard labour and physical strength are essential. To his second we answer that Eurasian associations have existed for over a hundred years, even though they are not examples of masterly organisation. The history of the Eurasians proves the third argument wrong. The fourth argument is true of many members of the community, but wiliness, unreliability, and untruthfulness are also characteristics of numerous Westerners. In answer to the fifth argument it must be regretfully admitted that lack of independence is a communal characteristic of the present-day Eurasian, but there is evidence that independence is not wanting in the new generation which is growing up.

The sixth argument is a nonsensical platitude, implying that only a white man may resign an appointment ' when his feelings have been hurt.'

As one who knows the methods of many white employers, I am only surprised that so many Eurasians stand what they do. The sort of

criticism which Eurasians have to suffer can be
judged from the seventh argument.

I may only say that Eurasian prostitutes[12] *are

_____

12   *EDITORS NOTE: According to Megan Stuart "Stereotypes
of Anglo-Indian women have proven as tenacious as they are contra-
dictory. The much quoted rantings of Nirad Chaudhuri in The Con-
tinent of Circe (1965) to do with unstable, promiscuous, degenerate
women, are the eccentric notes of an eccentric writer. Nonetheless,
Chaudhuri's editors at Chatto and Windus seem to have seen nothing
in need of revision when preparing subsequent editions. His wildest
comments reappear replete with his remarks concerning Anglo--
Indian prostitutes and "amateur practitioners". Beyond Kipling or
the self-projecting novels of bored colonial housewives, the image of
the promiscuous or otherwise sordid Anglo-Indian woman recurs.*

*Mircea Eliade's (1950) Bengal Nights contains several unsavoury
comments on the community at large and the "shallowness" of Anglo-Indian women in particular. Rumer Godden (1975), who might
be expected to offer a better interpretation in view of her lifelong
exposure to India, managed to create a superlative post-Independence
caricature in Alix Lamont the social climbing woman intent upon
hiding her origins in The Peacock Spring. This kind of representation might be simply dismissed except for an Anglo-Indian reality
pointing strongly in the opposite direction.*

*If a female Anglo-Indian stereotype were to be constructed it would
be influenced more by the convent- trained nurse, the loyal teacher
or office worker all of which contrast with perhaps the ghastliest
female stereotype of all: the Anglo-Indian girl trying to ensnare an
Allied soldier during World War II - at a time when thousands of these
women staffed medical and communications services throughout Asia
and beyond and their "feckless" brothers made up large contingents
in the RAF and other forces in every theatre of the War."*

comparatively rare anywhere in the East, while
the hordes of white inmates of brothels, who can
be procured for an average price of fifteen shil-
lings, are a serious problem of municipal administration. To the last argument I would reply
that the natives everywhere respect the Eurasians*[13], while the whites despise them because
they are subconsciously afraid of them.

It will now be admitted that the critics of the
Eurasian community have **grossly** exaggerated
the defects in its character; that while they
have often been right in describing its weaknesses, they have certainly been unscientific (if
not unfair) in not extending their examination
to causes. It is also evident that neither history
nor biology provides the slightest proof in favour
of the contention that the half-caste is inher-
ently inferior to either of his parents. It is true
a scientist wrote that "even a little admixture
of native blood seems to result in an individual
who possesses the bad qualities of both races."
But, while some biologists may agree with him,
the majority will feel that he had wandered too
far from the realm of systematic botany for his
opinions to be seriously considered.

---

13 *'Nearly a century ago Ricketts pointed this out to the Select Committee on the Affairs of the East India Company. (Stark,
Hostages to India, page 83).

Indeed, the scales of biological evidence clearly swing in favour of the theory that the carefully nurtured hybrid is superior to either parent. And those who hold this view in regard to human hybrids rightly believe that the inter-racial difficulties of the world will be solved by the development of mixed breeds, and that the removal of racial friction by marriage will ultimately lead to the peaceful occupation of the whole world by one composite race.

When the soap-box politicians of our day share with the mountebanks the ineluctable oblivion which awaits the uncreative mind, when the alarmists and old women of both sexes perish as all pettiness must perish, when international co-operation is recognised as a surer road to prosperity than repression and belligerency, when world-pride is recognised as more worthy than national pride, this vision of the Future will be recognised as truly prophetic. For the ' menace of colour ' exists only in the tortured minds of selfish capitalists and the unthinking rabble.

The Meekest and Most Despised of Men founded the greatest religion on earth. Perhaps in the centuries to come the despised half-caste will be instrumental in securing international amity

CIMMERII?

and prosperity.

So much for the far-distant Future. Let us return to the Present.

Chapter IX

We have said that as Christ founded the greatest religion on earth, so Eurasians may be the harbingers of international amity. In this connection it is an interesting digression to point out that even in the ancestry of the " Son of Man ' both illegitimacy and mixed blood can be distinctly traced.*14 The evidence is in the Bible itself.

The illegitimacy is proved by Matthew's genealogical table, in which he mentions Phares and Zara (i, 3), the unlawful twin sons of Thamar, who had " played the harlot' with Judas, her own father-in-law, and through him was * with child by whoredom * (Genesis, xxxviii, 13—30).

The evidence for Christ's mixed blood is also found in Matthew (i, 5—6): " and Booz begat Obed of Ruth; and Obed begat Jesse; and Jesse begat David the King." Now Ruth was of the

---

14 •I am indebted to Mr. H. W. B. Moreno for suggesting this chapter. I may add that it is not intended to be blasphemous, for the genealogical tables in the Bible are among its most subtle (if not strictly accurate) passages, and to point out that Christ had in Him the bloods of the lowest and the highest (this is disputed by Renan and others) is surely not blasphemy.

people of Moab, who were very distinct ethnolog-
ically and geographically from the people of Israel. This is shown in Ruth's own words (Ruth, i,
16) for whither thou goest, I will go, and where
thou longest, I will lodge; thy people shall be my
people, and thy God my God.

That Christ himself was particular about the
ethnological distinctiveness of the Israelites
is indicated by his words to the woman of Ca-
naan: "I am not sent but unto the lost sheep of
the house of Israel   it is not meet to take the
children's Bread, and cast it to dogs " (Matthew,
xv, 24—26).

When the so-called taint of illegitimacy and
intermixture can be traced in the ' King of Kings
', is it logical for His declared subjects to vilify
those of their fellow-men who cannot prove a
pure pedigree?

Chapter X

Satisfied with our contentions regarding the potential abilities of the Eurasian community, we must now face the argument that its biological foundations are unsound, that it will be unable to preserve its identity—while the barriers of race and country still exist.

A slight acquaintance with the mechanism of Mendelian heredity may appear to support this theory, but it breaks down upon critical examination. For example, an Eurasian male with the white factor dominant marries an English girl, or an Eurasian girl in whom the same factor exists. Their children will be predominantly indistinguishable in colour from English children. Per contra, the majority of the children of unions in which the dominant factor in both parents is Indian would need only to be clothed in native dress to be regarded as Indians. On the other hand numerous unions take place in which the dominant factors are opposites, in which case both dark and fair children would be produced.

As among natural animals so among men, however, the principle of selection is always inforce, and there is a natural tendency to select a mate approximating to one's own shade of the pigmentary spectrum. So there is an evident attempt in the Eurasian community to divide itself frankly into dark and fair, with the balance in favour of the fair. But in Eurasian families the colour of the children cannot be prophesied from the complexion of their parents; it often happens that a fair couple (in one or both of whom fairness is not really dominant) will have one or more brown children, or vice versa.

It will be obvious that the inheritance of physical characters in mixed races is exceedingly complex, but it is safe to say—and general observations on Eurasians bear this out—that the segregation and recombination of characters generally prevents a reversion to the pure strain of either parent.

A striking illustration of this fact is provided by various individuals of those Indian races who in former times came under the influence of the Greeks. For centuries they have been absorbed in the native stock, but the discerning observer can still easily distinguish their Greek inheritance.

Moreover, in considering the working of the Mendelian law in mixed races we have also to consider the environmental factor, which is generally inimical to absolute reversion to one or the other of the parent stocks. Blackness or whiteness does not make an Eurasian a native or an Anglo-Saxon.

However black he may be, the Eurasian stubbornly resists the submergence of his identity with the natives of the country, for he is proud of his Anglicised customs and his remote connection with the ruling race. And, however white he may be, it is seldom that an Eurasian, hampered as he is by economic distress and the cumulative effects of social prejudice, can successfully pose as a Britisher. The ties of the motherland are hard to severe, and sun-kissed relations (sometimes even one's own children) are so very difficult to conceal!

Nevertheless, a certain number of Eurasians do manage to include themselves with the Europeans, while a smaller number lose their identity in the maternal stock. But we may be assured that the Eurasian people, with their average yearly increase of two per cent, are steadily growing from year to year; that they will con-

tinue as a separate group, till that distant day
when the broken barriers of race and creed will
permit the men who recognise all the Earth as
their nation to reflect wonderingly on the follies
of their ancestors.

Chapter XI

We have seen that the biological foundations of the Eurasians favour their continuance as a separate group. Indeed, Prof. P. C. Mahalanobis, who for ten years has been concerned with an anthropological and biometrical study of the Eurasians of Bengal, believes that they represent a homogeneous group arc crystallizing out as a distinct racial entity—that they are a * race ' in the making.*[15] His views are supported by the genetic theory that constant self-fertilization of a heterogeneous group leads to eventual homozygosis.

Elsewhere, the natural vigor of hybrid groups of humanity has been strikingly demonstrated by the inhabitants of Pitcairn and Norfolk Islands in the Pacific. Little more than a century ago ten

15   *His analysis of the male stature of Anglo-Indians in Bengal (1922) clearly shows that they are a statistically homogeneous group, while Thurston's and Rangachari's earlier study of the Eurasians of South India (Castes and Tribes of South India, II, p. 218 c» acq., Madras. 1909) also indicates that Eurasians have many physical characteristics peculiar to them. In passing it is interesting to note that the more intelligent Eurasians are realising this. See, for example, Hobson, " Anglo-Indians and Communal Representation " in the Young Men of India, May, 1926.

CIMMERII?

English sailors, six Polynesian men and twelve Polynesian women, were compelled to take refuge on Pitcairn' Island, from where they eventually spread to the neighboring Norfolk Island. To-day, I believe, there is a flourishing community, unhampered and uncontaminated by racial prejudice, of more than one thousand individuals on both these islands.

As an argument against the continuity of the Eurasian race, the critic will be inclined to cite the case of the Luso-Indian community, but it is in reality a supporting argument. For, though the Luso-Indians have lost their European distinctiveness, they still retain, after five hundred years, a semblance of their original Portuguese customs; they still speak a patois of the Lusitanian tongue; and they are still as staunchly Catholic as the religious zealots who brought them into being.

They have in fact become a distinct ' race ' of the natives of India. It is unlikely, however, that the Eurasians will share a similar fate in the near future, for the Luso-Indians were totally deprived of contact with their Portuguese fathers, while even in India, where their political autocracy is clearly doomed, the British will never withdraw en masse.

The world has progressed too far for that; and Westerners will continue to trade there on a new basis. We may safely conclude, therefore, that the racial evolution of the Eurasians will be along different lines to that of the Luso-Indians.

Accepting the racial continuity of the Eurasians as an established fact, how may they improve their future status? The answer comes readily in two words: by Education. With a sound education, not the smattering of the Rs which pass for education in Eurasian schools, will come a proper appreciation of the other factors concerned in the general development of the community— sane political ideas, social and economic progress, physical improvement, real independence and a critical appreciation of values.

All this will take time. But indications are not

wanting which show that there is a small but growing body of Eurasians who are intellectually capable of guiding their people along the true road to prosperity; that the community is in a position to follow the doctrines dictated by organised common-sense is also becoming increasingly evident.*[16] It should be the duty, therefore, of all Eurasian men and women who can be teachers to devote every available moment of their lives to teaching.

The results, I prophesy, will astound the world. And of these patriots shall a new Derozio sing.

---

16   *In India, the impression created by the following publications of the Social Study Society of Calcutta, which have been written either by Eurasians or friends of the community, favors this argument. The papers in question are : Woolley's Some Problems of the Domiciled Community, 1912; Gilchrist's Survey of a Calcutta District, 1913; Chambers' Usury, and its Relation to Anglo-Indian Poverty, 1913; de Bois Shroabree's Practical Housing for the Anglo-Indian, 1913; Clifford's Facts and Figures and their Meaning, 1914; and Moreno's Anglo-Indians and the Housing Problem, 1917.

Chapter XII

What are the principles on which these disciples of emancipation shall base their efforts? As one who knows the Eurasian throughout the East, will offer these suggestions for what they are worth. The first plea, as I have said, should be for more education. The educational facilities in the East—and the further East we go the worse they are—available to the Eurasian are a disgrace to any humane legislation; they seem to be deliberately calculated to keep the half-caste in his place. Better schools, better teachers, more scholarships, more financial assistance must be demanded from the Governments concerned. School curricula must be re-organized to meet modern needs; greater economy of time and labour must be insisted upon; night-schools, vocational training centers, and opportunities for spare time study must also be provided.

But demands are not enough. The Eurasians must show the world that they are really in earnest by studying in their homes and by setting up their own educational institutions. In spite of their economic distress, there are sufficient wealthy

Eurasians {who could supplement their dona-
tions with public subscriptions) to make this
possible. In India and Malaya I know several
persons who, had they the burning patriotism
of a Booker T. Washington, could found a better
Tuskegee.

In the past Eurasians have not been unmindful
of education. Private schools and colleges existed
all over India, the most prominent being the
Parental Academy founded by J. W. Ricketts, to
which Capt. John Doveton, an Eurasian in the
Nizam's army, left an endowment of fifty thousand pounds.

The leaders of the community who, instead of
striving to increase the funds of the Doveton
College (as the Academy was later known), in
1916 recommended its abolition and the trans-
fer of the endowment to another school, should
hang their heads in shame. What the community
needs is a bigger and better Doveton College, a
college which, unimpaired by religious dogmas,
will impart a really sound and, if necessary,
free education, based on the latest researches
into the needs of the Men-to-Be. 1 asserts (and

EURASIANS AND THEIR FUTURE

I know that few Eurasians will understand my meaning) that no such college exists anywhere in the East. I am also confident that on its rolls would be the names of students coming from Colombo to Tokyo—and still further afield.

The next plea should be for Unity and Harmony. It is futile, wasteful and illogical for Eurasians to divide themselves into Anglo-Indians, Anglo-Burmans, Anglo-Malayans, and the like. Futile and wasteful because in their disabilities at least they form a composite group; illogical because the so-called Anglo-Indian may have no British blood in him (among other nations, the Dutch, Danes, Portuguese, Prussian, French and Flemish have contributed to the growth of the community), while the Anglo-Burman may be a Franco-Indian ! Moreover, the children of Indo-European unions are excluded from the Anglo-Indian community, an economic error against which the rapid growth of half-castes whose fathers are Asiatics provides impressive evidence. To the credit of the Eurasians of Burma it must be said that they have realised this, and that their definition of an Anglo-Indian is entirely liberal in this respect.

The psychologist will understand the tendency to

get away from the term Eurasian and its atten-
dant stigma of contemptibility, but the Eurasian
must be taught that the only way to conquer an
evil is to fight it, not to run away from it.

The term Eurasian (coined by the sagacious
Marquess of Hastings) is the most logical and
the most applicable. Its universal adoption
would have an unifying effect, the first step to
greater strength. For example, one Central Eurasian Association with autonomous branches
throughout India, Burma and Malaya, would
naturally be much more powerful, wealthy and
efficacious than are the present straggling Associations in these countries.

There is nothing to be gained, but much to be
lost, from this pathetic insistence on the "Anglo."
It has brought ridicule on the community; it has
strengthened its inferiority complex. Indeed,
who would not smile contemptuously when he
finds a responsible leader of the community say-
ing*[17] in impassioned words: " Britishers we are
and Britishers we ever must and shall be.

Once relinquish this name and permit ourselves

17 • See The Anglo-Indian Cause, issued by the Imperial Anglo-
Indian Association, Calcutta, 1898. The name of this Association
rightly drew on it the public sarcasm of Lord Curzon.

to be styled 'Eurasians', or 'statutory natives of India, and we become estranged from our proud heritage as Britishers." A stirring appeal to the multitude, but tripe to the sensitive constitution of the student. The Eurasians must realise that Eurasians they ever shall be, that a Bengalee dressed in a kilt does not become a Highlander.

It may be argued that in India the adoption of the term Eurasian would divorce the Domiciled European (the name is an obvious misnomer for a European domiciled in India would be a domiciled Indian) community, but owing to political conditions this is in any case inevitable and the number of domiciled Europeans who really identify themselves with Anglo-Indians at present is infinitely small, being practically confined to men whose wives are of mixed blood.

The Change of name should not alienate them. If fair Eurasians try to pose as Europeans, it can readily be understood that pure white domiciled families hesitate to join issue with the Anglo-Indians.

[These views have since been borne out by a letter (appealing for assistance in the compilation of the new electoral rolls for Bengal) dated

CIMMERII?

April 25, 1929, from the Chief Secretary to the Government of Bengal " To all Members of the Bengal Chamber of Commerce, Calcutta Trades Association and to all Government Offices," in which it has not only been ruled that Domiciled Europeans shall be classed in the European constituency, but that Anglo-Indians of pure European parentage on the father's side shall be similarly classed.

The latter ruling is so dangerous to the safety of the community that it should meet with universal protest. By it Col. Gidney would no longer be an Anglo-Indian but an Irishman, though his children (if he has any) would remain Anglo-Indians must be ruthlessly stamped out.

Eurindians are the chief offenders in this respect. It is a saddening spectacle to find Col. Gidney (for whose surgical accomplishments I have the deepest respect) crying for protection to Sir John Simon and his colleagues*[18]; it is no less pitiful to find Mr. Stark (towards whose

18 •See the Anglo-Indian Review, XVIII, No. 7, July, 1928, and XIX, No. 1, January. 1929. (" Memorandum of the Anglo-Indian and Domiciled Community of India submitted to the Simon Commission," and" Evidence before the Simon Commission "). The memorandum and the evidence were reported and commented upon (mostly adversely) in the Indian press towards the end of 1928.

EURASIANS AND THEIR FUTURE

scholarship I am equally reverent) writing in
his history of the Eurasians in India that " In
truth we are England's Hostages to India, and
they who give and they who receive hostages are
bound to regard them as a trust."

Let us away with such childish nonsense. Let us
teach Col. Gidney and Mr. Stark that protection
weakens a people; that it reduces competition,
increases inertia, and produces a false sense of
security. Moreover, the protected are always at
the mercy of the protectors ; they get only what
they are given; and they live under the constant
shadow of a political sword of Damocles. The
great truth must be learned that the road to
Eurasian emancipation lies not in supplication,
nor only in righteous demands for fair and just
treatment, but in developing themselves to be at
least as good as the other fellow.

67

Chapter XIII

As I have already hinted we can trace this whine for British protection, this inordinate pride in the British element in the Eurasian cocktail, to a very simple psychological reason—the desire common to most men to be on the winning side.

It is proved by the frequent and expensive deputations sent by the Eurasians of India to England in the last hundred years, and by their numerous .expressions of loyalty to the British Raj. So far back as 1881, an anonymous critic*[19] of the then recently formed Eurasian and Anglo-Indian Association pointed out that sixteen hundred rupees, which could have been more profitably employed, had been wasted on assuring Her Majesty Queen Victoria of the Association's loyalty. He quoted an unconscious philosopher who wrote : "I think it was unnecessary to spend Rs. 1,600 to tell Her Majesty that we are so very loyal. Her Majesty knows, as well as we Anglo-Indians do ourselves, that we dare not be dis-

---

19   * *Topics of the Day. No. 1. A Consideration of the Causes that Retard the Progress and Well-Being of the Anglo-Indian Community (Calcutta, 1881).*

loyal."

A veritable complex of weaknesses has been
erected on this supine attitude. Chief among
these are constant dependence on the benevo-
lence of the rulers (and a negative dissatisfac-
tion because they do not raise Eurasians from a
curry and rice diet to one of champagne and cav-
iar); the development of an intense colour prejudice within the community (which is patheti-
cally humorous to the thoughtful observer); the
almost entire lack of communal consciousness
{ and how can it be otherwise when Eurasians
are mostly ashamed of their birth}), leading to
a perpetual ambition in the dark to ' improve
the breed,' in the fair to join Anglo-Saxon Society—an ambition which when unrealized (or
unrealizable) involves justifiable ridicule, which
when successful weakens the strength, wealth
and status of the community.

It may be claimed by the white propagandist
that my psychology is wrong, that the real reason for the Eurasians' pro-white attitude is their
subconscious recognition of the intrinsic superi-
ority of the white races. The argument is based
on the personal interpretation of comparative
values; and I maintain, with thousands of oth-

ers, that the East is in no way inferior to the
West. And I am convinced that were Asiatic the
real rulers of their own countries, the Eurasians
would be even more pro-Asiatic than they are
pro-European to-day.

But be that as it may, the Eurasians must be
shown that their future lies with themselves.
They have been unfairly treated in the past, but
this does not give them the right to preferential
treatment in the present. They must insist, however, that in the right to eat the bread they earn
they are equal to any other community; they
must also insist on equal opportunities for earn-
ing that bread. And they must fit themselves to
take advantage of these opportunities.

In this they will never be generally successful
until they eliminate those primitive instincts
which stand between them and the development
of communal consciousness. When the Eurasians
are proud of being Eurasians, when they are
proud of being sons of the soil on which they
were reared, the problems of their race will have
been largely solved. For, with the right type of
communal pride will come the determination to
show the world that the community is second
to none; that it can hold its own with any race,

white or black. When this determination is born the rapid progress of the community will follow as surely as night follows day.

The petty politics of the passing hour may meet with temporary success. Petty politicians may even earn coveted ribbons by mega phoning their British heritage and their claims on the country of their fathers. But I am vain enough to believe that permanent emancipation can only come from toiling along the uphill road I have attempted to indicate.

After all we cannot live a lifetime in knicker-bockers. And even the dependent son of fond and financially secure parents can live at best a life of parasitic (and not altogether easy) ease. The son of parents who lack real stability, who regard him either with actual disfavor or an ungracious tolerance, can hope at most for the leavings of the parental table —when there is anything left. Need I stress the moral?

Chapter XIV

Who will be the pioneers of this New Movement in Eurasia? I answer unhesitatingly that they will be found, as in the last century the greatest Eurasians were found, among the younger element in the community. It is to its Youth that the race must look for improvement—that Youth who is slowly learning from the school-desk, from the playing fields, from the rigorous competition of his age, that success comes only from within.

The Eurasian girl is learning that a happy home, healthy children and social equality depends as much on herself as on her husband ;*[20] it is dawning on the prospective bridegroom that the home of his dreams depends on his ability to help his bride to realise and develop her new found ideals. These subconsciously assimilated truths must carry the community forward.

---

20   *It is a sign of the times that in the Anglo-Indian Citizen, May, 1929, Miss Mercia Heynes-Wood insists on a liberal, secular education for Eurasian women, and emphasizes the need for a knowledge of eugenics and other subjects concerned with the fulfillment of happy marriages and healthy (but few) children. She also stresses the important part which women play in the development of racial pride or otherwise.

And here and there will arise a Youth who has learned faster than his fellows, who will help to hasten the universal Awakening, who through life will bear these words like a torch in flame: " Play up, play up, and play the game." It is these youths who will be the teachers of the grand old doctrines of Self-Help and Mutual Aid.

They will be the critics of near-sighted politicians ; they will know that the ideals of to-day are the accomplishments of to-morrow; they will rise above prejudice and show the White World that the colour bar is a cruel, petty thing born of unreasoning fear; they will demand equality of treatment, opportunities and legitimate assistance, knowing that in their demands they have a Supreme Right—the right of the Men of the Future to ask of the Intelligence of To-Day.

Chapter XV

A nd a word to the White World. You have
brought this great mixed race into being.
Yet you have treated it always with indifference, usually with contempt, often with cruelty.
You have left it to grow like the wild plants of
a garden, to straggle untended where it would.
You did this because you were afraid, afraid that
your own progeny would usurp your supremacy.
You were wrong; foolishly, cruelly wrong.

What can you do now to better the plight of your
children? It is true you cannot undo the evil you
have done. It is too late to give them your entire protection. Indeed, it would be but another
wrong to pamper and spoil them, for they have
grown up and they must learn to help themselves. It is a perplexing situation. Yet, there are
some things you can do to help these Cimmerian
people to come out into the light—and live there
happily.

You can be sympathetic, encouraging, and just.
You can take an active interest in their uphill
climb; you can give them a hand when they
stumble by the way. But all this you can never

do until you realise, as the true thinkers of the
world, even your world, have realised, that
there is no more evil thing than race prejudice;
that (in the words of H. G. Wells) " it justifies
and holds together more baseness, cruelty, and
abomination than any other sort of error in the
world." With centuries of culture behind you,
with modern philosophers all around you, is it so
very difficult to realise this?

Are you blind to the growing sense of injustice
in the dark races, their growing determination
to free themselves from your autocracy? Listen
to these words of E. B. du Bois, one of the most
moderate of Negro thinkers: "What then is this
Dark World thinking? It is thinking that, wild
and awful as this shameless war was, it is nothing to compare with that fight for freedom which
black and brown and yellow men must and will
make unless their oppression and humiliation
and insult at the hands of the White World
cease. The Dark World is going to submit to its
present treatment just as long as it must and
not one moment longer."

These words are pregnant with a grim meaning.
They mean also that the menace of colour will be
a menace—and a very real menace—only so long

as you make it one. So, it is not only fairness to the Eurasian which demands a readjustment of your outlook on the universe.

Which will you heed? The wisdom of your philosophers or the ebullitions of your fools.

AFTERWARD

Tetzel the Bohemian, gazing for the first time on Cape Finisterre, exclaimed in wondering pessimism : " My God, what is the end of all this?" His words have permeated my thoughts throughout the penning of this essay. So, believing it as logical for a writer to include his final reflections in an afterword as it is to express his preliminary views in a foreword, I have added these lines.

What, indeed, is the end of all this? Will the Eurasian community really develop, will it really usher in a new world-consciousness? The preceding pages are after all mainly a survey of past history, an exposure of unfair criticisms, and a defence of potentialities. The stern fact remains that the Eurasians are a backward, indifferently educated people. *[21] Will one book, a thousand books, stimulate them into activity, and secure

---

21   EDITORS NOTE: This is a stereotype according to research by M Stuart Anglo-Indian literacy and contribution to primary education, as proved- by India's network of 250 "Anglo-Indian" schools and have long surpassed the rates of other Indian communities (d'Souza, 1976; Varma, 1979).

CIMMERII?

for them their rightful place in the world?

Perhaps not, but I am saved from absolute despair, because I know the seeds of progress are deeply implanted in human breasts—and Eurasians are no exception to the rule. And, as we pass, we who write can pick the grubs from the growing shoot.

I am saved from despair because I know also that captious critics and petty politicians will come and go, but the Eurasian people will plod slowly onwards, secure in the knowledge (perhaps knowing it not) that the dogs bark but the caravan moves on.

The Books in The Anglo Indian Heritage Series are

Britian's betrayal in India: the story of the Anglo indian Community. by Frank Anthony

ISBN 1-84356-010-0

These Are The Anglo-Indians by Reginald Maher

ISBN 1-84356-012-7

Hostages to India: The Life story of The Anglo Indian Race by Herbert Alick Stark

ISBN 1-84356-011-9

Cimmerii? Or Eurasians and Their Future by Cedric Dover

ISBN 1-84356-013-5

They are avaiable via Amazon and all Good bookshops Worldwide

----

The Anglo Indian Heritage

The books are called the Anglo Indian Heritage books as they chronicle the rich and colourful history of the Anglo Indian Community. This small community has had outstanding achievements at every level of society for hundreds of years but that record of achievement has been hidden, passed over or co-opted as British and Indian History. These Books are an attempt to fairly represent the history of the community by works by Anglo Indians themselves.

If you would like us to publish your book or

If you would like to distribute our books please e mail us at our contact address:

wallenberg.press@gmail.com

List of International Federation Members

Noel Murphy & Debbie Sequiera
The Anglo-Indian Guild of Victoria (Inc)
PO Box 269
North Braybrook - Melbourne
VIC 3019
Australia
Telephone: 03 9364 9054

Mrs Joy Gasper
Denzil Bruce (Host)
The Australian Anglo Indian
Association (Inc)
32 Fernwood Square
Padbury - Perth, WA - 6025
Australia
Telephone: 08 9344 1228

Yolande Gibbons
The Australian Anglo Indian
Association (NSW) Inc
PO Box 156
St Clair, Perth - NSW
2759 - Australia
Telephone: 08 9256 4909

Mrs Jenny Welsh
Anglo Indians in Touch
3852 Seebring Crescent
Mississauga, Ontario
L5L 3X7
Canada
Telephone: 0011 1 905 820
4785

Janice Emmett
Anglo-Indian Association of
Canada
2535 Bayview Ave
Ontario - M2L 1B1
Canada
Telephone: 0011 1 905 775-
3580.

Mr Joss Fernandez
The Anglo-Indian Guild (Regd)
St Mary's Orphanage
8, 2nd Cross Dcosta Layout
Bangalore - 560084
India
Telephone: 0011 91 80-
25361414

Harry Maclure   Anglo Indian in the Wind
India - Bangalore
Telephone: 0011 91 - 44 -
42080058.

Dr Geoffrey Francis
The Anglo-Indian Association of
Southern India
1/2 Ponniamman Koil Street
Egmore
Chennai - 600008
India –
Telephone: 001191-44-
28413937.

Ms.Philomen Eaton

The Calcutta Anglo-Indian Service Society
c/- Lawrence DeSouza Home
138 Lenin Sarani
Kolkata - 700013
India
Telephone: 0091 33 22446185

Telephone: 0011 44 208 998
5137.

Mr David Samaroo
The United Kingdom Anglo-In-
dian Association
1 Lynton Avenue
West Ealing
London - W13DEA
Unitede Kingdom

Printed in the United Kingdom
by Lightning Source UK Ltd.
123142UK00001B/128/A